Nicholas Lea

Nicholas Lea

EVERYTHING IS MOVIES

Ottawa 2007

Everything is movies
© 2007, Nicholas Lea

Cover design by Tanya Sprowl
Layout by Jef Harris and Jennifer Mulligan
Edited for the press by rob mclennan

printed and bound in Canada
by Custom Printers, Renfew, Ontario

Chaudiere Books
858 Somerset Street West
Main Floor
Ottawa, Ontario
K1R 6R7

www.chaudierebooks.com
email: info@chaudierebooks.com

Library and Archives Canada Cataloguing in Publication

Lea, Nicholas, 1982-
        Everything is movies / Nicholas Lea.

Poems.
ISBN 978-0-9781601-7-3

        I. Title.

PS8623.E25E84 2007   C811'.6   C2007-902201-4

For Bill and Denise Lea

Contents

Monocle on 9

Song writhing 31

Dummies wonder 45

Everything is movies 83

Monocle on

Monocle on

I'm afraid to start.

The world is mostly Good&Evil.

I'm afraid to start.

Dear You

You'd be jealous.

To be here in the unyoked
momentary blindness. Not
missing giggling past the porn
store or arguing the missed
jurisdiction of our coolth—saying:
I'm going to sight my sets a little
higher.

Here,
blossoms drop bombs on the un-
soaked notion of a sick ocean,
a frolic in the zucchini field
under
a tough
sun.

Forget finding obsolete teeth
in the street: fresh-blooded and flesh-
flecked.

Scratch rescinding into night, pushing
our children to the thrum of something
vicious.

No stopping to browse The Terror Shop:
Thick in the Business of Innocence.

In this battered matter (of fact) your
envy would brim, spill over—no . . .
vehicle your every whim.

Midrift

Still, be sung.

Dislodge the hodgepodge of love
in you

and say: *act your social class*,
in a deadening of light—

so polite and scarred
and starstuck—so unlike

the altered state of the apostate matron
who, too choosey for us
                           lay imaginaries,

fashioned and mounted her own kind
of sky: fireless and never-hanging.

Still . . .

be snug in the geographical mist.

Your lost soccer ball floating
slow and doughy in a moat of canal.

Epic

Out the sibilant corner of afternoon
light, she arose from a nap.
The moon grew a lung. Our hero
at this time is half asleep but fully
realized. Here enters a flock
deep in its synchronies. Our hero
records. A comet turns back. Our
hero gets whipped with meaning.

One must wonder whether our
hero will learn to unnerve her body,
whether the clocks will stop gest-
iculating, night live up to its inane name.
Naima plays. Our hero purchases some
Spun Thunder even though unhungry.
She will begin to crave grapefruit and
wrath, shave her legs with a credit card.

Wait! Our hero misses the epiphany. This
is called Nihilism. We think. We often
take chances on words, burn our thumb-
nails, *bic*-style. This grit is too imported.
We will soften on principle. Our hero
will not entertain even the vaguest notion
of a sick ocean, she is at home with her can
of flaked tuna. Our hero prepares to slay

the monster within. She dulls her blade
in the grass, finds love instead. Our
hero is preoccupied with chance and
hardcore celebrity. Our hero must won-
der whether the clocks will stop contesting—
must wander wander wander—until there is
pseudo-Hope. No more policing the inner-life.

Some reasons the poems of Marcus McCann are at once un and ceremonious

Try to weave through this, this
congested vesper, begun not-
on-schedule and maladroitly performed
(of course). This is the way it's done:
fumbling to some delicater eloquence,

right?

Here it is: the fervent journaling:
a rash of simulacra. A scrimmage
of swapped chakras to re-
group on a single eyelash. ~~A poem is~~
~~an obliqueing reason, a claim bailing out.~~

Oh, and ceremony. What of that?
The precious procession, the snicker-
ing altar boys, the list-
less furrows, rowed and proverbial

This . . . this profane oscillation is less a life-
style than a poem joking about its own
thinness. But this

"This"   is *no lacking matter.*

Aquifer

Not a *pas de tout,*
Bonhomme, a

cab, vestibular. A
truck, his little white pick up
line. Dammit practical,
goddammit raincan.

He's climbing in, hick, cupped
a Cornwall prestige.

Said salty, heard
saltier. Might as well

be the weather: a done
deal, the light left marbling
on the mac tac. Or was it
Formica under the crocheted curtain?

Decided no, later
hell no.

Adjustment was a skin on the sticky dash
arranging a jean leg, the clutch. He never saw the
sidewalk, maybe there was none.

(And

just so you know, there was never
any animosity between him and me, never
anything. Believe me I'd tell you.)

Unnatural speeds

for Jesse Ferguson

First,
there's standard poise, the
standards. A friendship like
music. It's otherwise stock
perception, or somehow
harnessing the jargon. And
during all this the ice is melting.
A gradual melting that must relate
to time—so—*time* is melting, or,
melting is time. The inflection is
unclear. Hoped you could clarify, get
back to me.

First, there's no brainy sobriquet
for it. Nothing so cute. A violin
is skating (in
circles), another joins in, they
hold hands, and then another, and
another . . . all in order
to unbraid our
already twisted sense. Our world-
view. In time,
a tin-shrill chorus of bells will follow.

Do you already see the theme
of music, music and *ellipticality*?
It's really all about timing: swing
or waltz, it's temporal. First, we
coerce the circus out of town,
embrace a more-than-willing fate
that shepherds us towards the butterfly
chase (*pssst, we're not ready yet, where's
your net?*)

I had a dream about a town:
the trees were uncanny, the plot was knotty.
First, I was sucked through a jet engine and survived
to tell the story, do the interviews: gave them
with a Spanish guitar, strumming flamenco-
style after each tragic delivery, with tears.

But first, you were there and
the ice was
almost
completely
melted and that made a huge
statement about time
and its illegitimate funnelling.
There was only one tiny island left
as big as the world as at
first. We waded,
catching with our bare hands the last butterflies
with no intention of eating
them. And there was music. We
can't forget music.

Pin cushion

The art is in the pin cushion.
There's fervour and then again
there's fervour. Her knees knock,
are known to gnaw, are gnarled and
spilled with miso soup. She is cold

in the darkest grove, with its myriad
ink stains: red ink, like blood, but
good blood, benevolent blood. Take
cover. *Please leave your network
at the door*, this is a place of respite
from eachother. We call it community,
but only because it looks good on paper.

We've reasoned our Self into the jar, now
we travel. Jess blinks and disappears,
Julian bites his thumb at the snowplough.

Something must be electric—it fucking
must be! You finish tickling the Misfit,
excuse yourself to pee. *Generally,*

the TV will rule. And Basically,

what shines is what will inevitably sprout.

Sun shakes hands with moon

Contact the grape-
fruit. Shake
the centrifuge solid. It's

time for declaratives—time
as *appropriator* time
to forgive the vacuum its unswerving

vehement. Then,
maples tend to talk, consort
a line about your faces, various.

Bob Dylan or Vlad the Impaler?

(Please don't make me choose).

Though it's no coincidence, mistake.
A shadow will gladly guide you through
the lake of needles

when contracts are written in
split atoms, rock
misnomered.

Tableau vivant

The fragile-not-frail pray,
prey heavily, steadily in front
of the no-eyed providers. Will
dis-tills as *you* distil—stand
still, still in place, your
choice place. Still:

pillow fights are a two-
way street. At night we go
to sleep with ghost potential;
a fact lost on all

the recalcitrant creature
life: the indiscriminate killing
within. But

just remember to stay still
life—terrible and resonant

(no—beautiful, muted).

Sin new

It was during the après map, after
the series-disaster: the wind's
urinal cake smell, how everything
went yellowtinge, the *eco purge*. We've
all been there or here twice before.

Where silhouettes intensify. My
headache worsens. I reach
for new mist-sensation, discover the news,
totem-atoned, fluttering around on
dragonfly wings: paper-thin, but
natural, at last.

Be your opposite

So there's Shield between us, so what.
So it's snow-covered, muted by white—
who cares. There
are words: spare-
but-unrestrained, and
I've become resolute to slow étude.

There's a whole heart there.

Tell me who squired the inner-child
home, in the dark: *crunch,*
saw. Tell me (be law-
less) who twisted (*Indian burned*)
the masculanist's wrist. Tell me,

is it mauve enough?

The winter air bites with mice teeth,
my face paints its own blood-graffiti.
I can be vicious sometimes, can turn
exquisite fingers. If the corporeal

gives a paltry gesture, only
ghosts will react. Sad. And so
there's vast patches of snow between us.

I don't know how the light bulb works.

I'd like to learn.

Catholic moment

How, cathartic, your arms
are wrapped around me like
seatbelts. How your head
is half in my chest, your breaths
inflating my lungs. How you
drip, drop from your tail-
bone. How in this
sedate derangement of sleep,
i.e. the dark, you somehow
furrow your skin, goosebump
mine.

Animalsleep

In
-hale: large gulp of helium
sand in the toes, effluvium strand
-ed—the vary sleep-afflicted, in
-flicting a certain tangential silly.
A floral drill; your father's absent
gatherings: 43 hairs, 50 sinks, trinkets;
1 or 2 snowflakes for posterity.

Their (the heirs) favourite fair ride re
-called, never coming back, everseason.

:

Ensued gloom. As terrible a result.
Terrific rift-imaginings. All over. All
metabolism—   over.

And it occurs, forwards for
-ward looking the bleaker tree
canopy, and when you you fine
ally serious. Severe the tiering.

The *yup* of some beneviolent
matrices: a woolly enclosure:
a blame-sonnet to the privileged
but poorly attired—

:

And finally your inner-basement, live there.
Or wrap the mattress, cake the trolley
-wall where there is no more traces—
era sure.
              Decline the im
-pulse to forgive the drivel-image. In

fact, forgive it, if its brilliant start.

Postures

Burning sniveler:

Be grave of mien.
Be the goat too close to the toaster.
Turn your neck 180 degrees, pretend like it's nothing.
Sniff and sob when you hear the wonderful
news, then wax iconoclastic. Play your fated
part in the shattering of exclamatory
worlds.

Broad believer:

Never get too attached to the Commune.
Find the nerve of the peach. Spell your
name in the snow, but furtively, and preferably
by moonlight. Play those nylon strings
like they're steel or something.

Insane Pustule:

Find your self-surprising twang. Scrap
with your darned harmonizer when she
begins to upstage. Never mind the coin-wash
in your mind, your mind's eye's recessive
trait escaping for good. Look up. Look up:
"elliptical."

Flying jar:

Follow your heart to the
freight
train's
last
car.

Transubstantiation

A spent dog laps
tragic at the gravel floor.
The stone picks up steam. I am
the exhausted dog that lapses
in the sad gravel, while the old
stone throws steam.

Prayer

I am the backbone of the sun—
I am the tolerable sin—
I am a half-wiped whiteboard—
I am the canoe hit the iceberg—
I am Silt Head—
I am the regrettable haircut—
I am the apartment airing out—
I am the sequestered question—
I am the bad bad battlefield—
I am the Bear on the Delhi Road—
I am the neighbours having sex at noon—
I am the cat, thick in sleep—
I am the alien's fanciest probe—
I am uninspired times—
I am the heart on fiddle, the brain on bodhran—
I am the vortex's signature silhouette—
I am the orb outside itself—
I am the lifestyle change—
I am ambiguous screams—
I am ultimatelycompounded—
I am the sound of rain on a hamburger—
I am a bell on the floor, rubber wind chimes—
I am unfinished business—
I am routinely unreligious—
I am late for work—
I am the plant name that escapes me—
I am left of the Left that's left of the Left—
I am a spinning plate plate plate—
I am the personified abstraction—
The Song, writhing.

Song writhing

1.

is it just me
or the many
few who seem to
exaggerate a great
shaking?

2.

the stone circus is left town   moved on to the next county to
warp the young minds with its freak geology   it's all in the
heavy siltified timing what makes the show a hit   the medley
caught fondling the haze by the bank   your visions
unaccounted for   what is a trail really   a human tear through
wilderness   a beleaguered theme park in the thick of it
somehow the questions tire and the spectacle implodes   we
follow the myth to neither here nor there   forget for the life
of us how to shoe gaze   go back to the tragic lapses that
swim like fish through the air

3.

funny how your eyes are lips
shifting in and out
of pink light   how
single is split into a log
pile
stack
of
digestible cookies
on the baby
          tray of your palm

4.

evil seeks special treatment
in the downright even-
ing of this evening

wants to trip down
memory
lame   get right
                        pissed
reminisce

then forget like it's a sport or
something equally hobbyist

5.

forget how the thing went down   forget the phantom pianos
leased by pre-natal prodigies   forget this period of extreme
colour   forget the blades of rain come   gone   forget my
fault-lined museum   forget the coughing moon   the fledgling
night diver   forget what taught you to tie your thoughts to
lures of youth

6.

the former is the ladder
stilting our life

7.

all of the sudden the hours became ours   the wind a polite
molester version became fact fact back to version our
bourgeoning a blooming patch of cacti   sun stumbling on
the lens   we drank from our shoes in the semi-dew   took big
dollops of maple sap from the sand   just embrace the wicked
village you said   take it out from the inside you said   I wake
you and you come fumbling from your torpor and make us
breakfast

8.

this
ruffled blanket of
lips drifts
     and
        dips
          and
        drifts
     and
   dips
     and
       drifts
          and
          dips
          and
        drifts
     and
   dips
 and
drifts
and
dips
     and
    drifts
     and
       dips
        and
         drifts
        and
     drips
     drips
     drips
     drips
     drips

     drips

     drips

     drips

9.

when this is said to be hymnal in its approach   when the
lock-jaw moment rises and sticks   when fall falls but the falls
unfall   when we drip mysticism   when our arches collapse
when we feel unthinkingly   when thought ought not to be so
congruous   when sinking isn't such a bad idea   when motion
is miles from come ocean   when when went unwanting
when the moon was yours uniquely   when it sounded like a
dog got hit   when the mothership rescinded   when the car
alarm medley'd   when you formed when formulating the
question   when each trope choked   when the leaf yellowed
under sunlight   when we are *fizzy with sedatives*   when the
fawn on the road is exquisite but not majestic   when crow
leaves her work   when the tourists are getting restless   when
riverbank meets piggybank   when the paperclip saves the
ship   when the stigma's lifted slightly   when the catalogue
clogs   when the onslaught of progress is too furious   when
we entertain ourselves with meditations   when this is said to
be hymnal in its approach

10.

for Gord Downie

there's no song here
no song home alone
there's no song
no song on timing
no no song here
no song on its own
no song a song writhing

11.

silly question

let it live in the statued past
with all the fond hauntings

Dummies wonder

Vainglorious

The gelid crystals glaze the half-lake, amaze
the needled heads of winter. The membrane
wreaks havoc. Its manifestation: a tasteless joke
about the blind reading the blind. A gag
with attitude; a sulky miner: dustful, bleeding
from the eyes. What opacity!

What's opacity if the jobs have forsaken
us, the guarded guardians fish-hooked
to desire? We scale a muddy atoll, not an is-
land, but an atoll, trolling, not patrolling
the practically-black afternoon. We orbit,
revanquish . . .

incite our deepest violence, not because we want
to, but because we're allowed.

Have you ever killed yourself?

Something intersecting
is happening: alien
visitations, strange
village rituals, a communal
squashing.

As the moon-toothed
rooftops start bleating, oozing
fat shadows, secreting all the sad
that sleeps and limps inside. It's enough

to make one want to live beneath the sea—
beneath the creaky floorboards that
drizzle dust every time someone walks
across above.

When you get it
let me in on the joke: the ciphered
word etiolating slowly, by degrees—
so as to really drive that fact home,
really rub it in.

When you get it

tell me the singing outcome
from all Its stagnant machinations.

Its visible love.

Crowded out

There can't possibly be
a need for this: this

unadulterated swarming.
The girders are rusty as grave-

yards and the picture frame,
so pleasantly tilted.

It's time we honour Something
(me in my venerated phases).

Don't shrug!

The world is more than dishes and
miscarriages, you know . . . don't

believe Nietzsche. What's he ever
done for the garden? Observe

this houseplant as it either wilts or
blooms . . . you see: Magic.

And try to understand that fascism
is just a fad. The way the moon

ululates or the star sizzles.

Pilgrim aging

I've seen the *hee hee* in he
who will forever be a breast
pocket, was always and is
awesome.

A catheter in its seventh finest
mo(ve)ment.

Regret could fill a space helmet.

The rogue spells
everything lowercase: a case
can be made.

Daniel saved me from the barn
floor, so I broke his sword and
fled back home like a little
twister.

Continuations . . . continuing
living even though we lack
~~a certain vital~~ tragedy. Light.

Surrogate. Colour. Surrogate
colour: a dishrag on the floor.

Pointing at something.

I've failed to keep the romance
alive: I'm deeply deeply sorry.

The forest is really a shell.

Avatar

I shall never want or need
Any other literature than this poetry of mud

- John Ashbery

When we try to pry
the stick. When the mud's grip
outdoes the sun. The field
was flooded by torrent, our clipped
hope distopia-ed in seconds.

The grabby wind
currents the opaque pane of water,
shoves dry tubers in its random
directions.

The history of this sprig . . .

a querulous encryption too
occult for even your grandmother's
cleverest archaeology; a mirroring
no yoga-moment could ever refract, illuminate.

Throwing hay from barn roofs is no
consolation—
the rain-veined knoll, the gold that shoots
through everything,
is water on your eardrums—

is a contest of wind and indifference.

It is not

unlike spinning tires in slushy mud.
The maximum allowance of honey
in hand. The wood's stoves prolong
this bondage (this fixedness to *this*),
unvintage the serious bottles. What
was it again—what did you call it:
a garden of crestfallen embers not
bothering to blow on themselves
for survival? We are unconcerned.

A then-ascendant fact is crumpled
and tossed in the gully. We denounce
the dénouement or the duende or what-
ever clever escape, dun the scene for
orchestral variety. The hills rust.

We walk on fall'd rot.

Maxfield Road, Wakefield, Qc.

Going Theory

The pond chops a small
wave in wind. And always
you return to *the human*.

Losted concertina

The complex children pilgrimage. They wade the marrow of tundra, burn the money they earned or stole for survival reasons. Where they are headed is not important at this juncture, the point is they move.

The point is they are moving unusually fast for such little and unskilled pilgrims. There is no climax to speak of, no teleological reaching. No conga line. No brassy waltz. There is only rootlessness: the endless nomadics. There is no flight.

See them faction and dismantle faction and dismantle and cluster again. See one fall in love, the other hate intensely.

The difficult children bleep and rupture, their wails hollowly thrown in the sheer air; their wandering still on. A signal is breaking up.

The uninitiated

Don't say you're not familiar.
Say you're *uninitiated*. Say
the pulse of this heat is gregarious,
fleet (but only in botany terms).

A mirthy breathing sings
in and out in and out in and out in . . . .

Are you really **alone** when
the grass grazes your face in sunlight—
with its singing insects,
the gleaming bracelet,
the energy pill,
the militant ticks,
the monastic distance,
cloud formations,
field mice moiling,
the soil's electricity,
the pioneer foundation,
the various wings,
the salt mixed with water mixed with urine,
a leafy heap,
the pearls of wisdom,
the debated atom,
the aggregate jest,
the gist of it,
the ghost amalgam,
the gleaming bracelet,
the violent breeze,
the unfair advantage,
the gleaming bracelet,
the ecology of boxes,
the gleaming bracelet,
a gleaning bracelet?

Mixed feeling

I

The walls are factory stitched
with skinny thread, nearly
invisible. The door is a v-neck
sweater.

And all the portholes of the world
are opening—(but for four nano-
seconds only).

Welcome to the frigid dynasty:
this quivering grove, a stiff-mudded
axiom. They have anticipated your
return, calling you the *earth-bound
strategist's second favourite son.*

       Be not afraid.

Of course you're not, silly me.
You've been steeling yourself for years.

II

Did I say
the walls are stitched?
               (What was I thinking)

The walls are memory-foam, except
without the memory; except
without exceptions, dire
appraisals.

III

I thought I said *the door was a v-neck sweater*,
not a liminal collision of Purpose
and purpose?

IV

Wait. I said *welcome*, didn't I? I said welcome.

New illumination

After *Untitled, 2006*, by Gregory Crewdson

It's the never-sacred bleeding
into a big underneath. You plunge
your arm
down
the gutter, search in-
visibly for the lost good stuff, sweep
your fingers blind on the muck floor
for old shards
of star.

All the swell

A breeze off the lake—petal-shaped
Luna-park effects avoid the teasing outline
Of where we would be if we were here.

- John Ashbery

Trying, though quarter-heartedly, to otherwise
Hide, herd the long cloud pageant off the elec-
Tric isthmus. I vie with the metal surges, deke
A breeze off the lake—petal-shaped

And pain-sailing. Some body's seaweed is edifying
The driftnets. A harmonium takes the podium
Of sedated debate. Our jobs become us. And those
Luna-park effects avoid the teasing outline

That stashes horizon in panties, before shuffling
Through Customs. I touch the touchstone but feel only
A tickle at the back of my throat. No gold afterthoughts
Of where we would be if we were here.

I owe

Look
at the sad king slumped
in his throne. See the stooped
outcome, coming together,
coalescing. We've found no
ways of reducing, no way
to unvolumize the life: the
unfair interview, the nude
portrait, unconsented. A mutant
lily pad wades unwanting, mocks
the kid on the bank with the hand-
ful of rocks. And the last match
always never works.

We are soft
in the cornfields:
a stalk-choked world. Soft
in the void noise of sunshine.
Verity astride grey: the garbled
words of warning, the children's
literature dissected. We're soft. Soft
in the necessary, in the pornography
of asking. The purporting mystic
spending money on throwaway
furniture and exotic teas.

Ornament egg

To quell
the stilled head, learn
leaf-by-sordid-leaf, the
bronzed know-
ledge.
If the cold is too-furious
today, scarf yourself
and be swift.
I'll find the rusted truck-
turned-flower
you said might be
in the defunct quarry. I'll
ferry your hope—hope
the heavy weeds have over-
taken: the reclaim begun.

If it's lost, please,
take issue with the proto-
Realist mob outside
your shadowy back
stoop.

In bloom

What happened to the old
scorched hotel? Now
semi-empty: a big storage
room they call *dead space*—
infested (now) with clothy
memories, plasmatic ghosts
at a tattered table smoking expensive
cigarillos and drinking tawny
port.

A serious amassing
of the overused, the now-un-
wanted.
        It's like this glass
of cranberry juice, these salt&pepper
shakers: the purloined
provisions of another beach-read
moment, another plastic
            container
melting, oozing wax-like.

Anotherdiamondcluster.

        Bring in the trees, some
paint—re-invent the font. Make it
sexier than it's ever been.

        And whatever you do, don't
pity the hindered visionary when she
sees her new work in an old light.

Patterns of distribution

An awkward word
heard half-

spat on the branch of your arm. Are
you for real, when you blend

thin with shimmer?

If you're a Jungian

Suppose you noticed our actions
weren't ever artless, blithe, and
actually contracted: a comic pose with
a snowman, ignoring the week's heap
of laundry, daunted secretly.

Suppose the mission isn't clear, not even
in your head or your head's head or your head's
head's head. And, headed the wrong way, suppose
you drove
all
night
in the rain, garnering nothing: not a burnished
side-thought, an aside to send you swerving.

Suppose the biodiversity in this ditch
is simply clingy pages, pieces of
anon energy; the surmounted gall
of an acquaintance versus an old friend pouting
in her sleep, dreaming on fine
night air.
                Suppose

the whole thing turned out to be Psyche's
digital watch, cracked, wet on the inside, and
bleeding
            liquid

        crystal.

I never understood the difference

between object and subject, never
guessed the gestures that poured
floorward like sun. The periods that finalize,
infantilize our ageing rearrangements.

Some get stuck, snared.

Some get ephemeral.

I blur and opaque, casually
crane my fragile histories, packed
in a giant crab-net, thick, only to
writhe wraithlike and kick
their exotic limbs
in the air.

I don't know . . . maybe I'm feeling
sentimental right now, maybe in a day
I'll say something stock on the stars.

They live us.

They're buried in the belly's membrane.

Post who

No need to (a)mend your heady vengeance
(a ragged cloud-herd moseying on to: elsewhere)

or build it stilted. It's okay: the brittle rib cage
draws the brain's cartoons. This isn't navel

gazing by the Lake District. It's a windowless
chill come from a desert of question marks.

Have you ever put your eye an inch before the dirt
and left it there? You should—it's the New Sublime.

Watch as the dew turns virulent. Watch (violently)
the landed atom. No, it isn't super-elitist to assume

the drifter-plume-of-smoke is trying to keep it together,
the annexe, self-dismantling.

In those previous evenings, those reptile trials,
the alarmist's mystification undoes the surgery:

a laughing matter composing the butternut squash—
substantiating our balustrades of bliss.

"no sunbeam ever lies"

What they call *soft experience* witnesses
itself the most motivated invigilation. We are
what we call *eachother*—unless
what's invisible cripples by degrees. And what
they call whippoorwill's opinion is merely
an esoteric throat,   nothing more deep than that,
We assure you.

Let the words give berth.
Let it opine, shout   *drachma*! for no reason

in the forest of trees (*of course the forest of trees*).

Negation composes the poesy of indecision   or incision—
is a dredged tenderness,
an iconoclast's last bastard gasp. It's all

the nonsense verse your dream is glued
to: Christmas jingles brought to their penitent knees,
the grassy green under duress,   again. Again,

under duress   the grassy green
under the trumpet, once again, of duress.

Enter elbow

I

And you mock the automatons . . .
while stillness freaks in a tin-sheet
shed stocked with sundry lumber
an old chest full of sixties toys: vintage
blessings.

Where's your compassion,
adrift in weakness—your thinning
miracle-ability? Remembering
then almost-forgetting the red ban-
danna, the overalls, the army ruck-
sack of sherry and ham sandwiches?

The vistas?
The *scene*?

The alien   plain?

II

And so the non-smoking queen
is banished, vulcanized. O how
I
poeticize
my villainies! Loose the joist
with lip-invention. How this will re-
mind me of the echo-effects of a vacant
grain silo. Phenomena. *That* will be
my reference

point.

The sum-wonderment in this list
of happening.

Read: veil of haze

Is what I did irreparable; did
I not fight (with fervour) the fabled
virus? Are the many
few inseparable? The manic crackle
of a rowboat—moored and self-
elegant—on a rodeo of wave.

Did I not shout *Metaphysics is all Sky*!
in order to assuage the old Germanic
plumber (mid-wrench) in his most knowful
pose?

Of course I did! I did

flesh the moon from its hail of vase . . . .

I'm too pretty for this job

Each concrete vacillation fissures
the next.   Invents verbs.

It's so silent. The room is filled
with warm gel, suspending us. Grave
yards melt like ice in a pint glass.

The forced air, abruptly stopped—

making this new silence even louder.

Surely,
by now the crust has shifted at an abominable
speed. Surely,

we read too much into it, splitting
our lips, blistering, etc.

Discovering our deepest grief sad-
dled, strapped to the rumour-disaster, we
radiate. We have no choice.

Illumination is in-

evitable as the milky surgery
being performed by the moths.

I'm fizzling out. The room

reconstitutes.

The emergency is antique,

technically ornamental.

Vital ORgans

The miracle whispers, *what's
the status?* and flees pell-mell
before a response is possible.

There's an unsettling cough coming
from the kitchen at unnatural speeds.

It's the impossible degrees keeping
the monotone, filching the refracted
circles that daub the walls.

Prudent planning sings, *Break-fall
into my Baby's Arms*, while the clock

bombinates its philosophical opposite.
The miracle gets lost in a bromidic mood.
The miracle plays <u>two</u> scales on the lute at

barely-audible volumes. Somewhere there
is a weeper saturating something thin

and pliable. Somewhere there is a weeper
saturating something thin and pliable.

Let us compare mythologies

Oh no, I don't remember that:

attacking magic, its various forms,
functions, famous hang-outs. Saying
the past happened in a field of crucified
missives. A balding shed of corroborative
imaginings, collaborative projections.

No, that's not how it happened:

happened oftener than thought-wrought
retellings, crooked penmanship. The cat
all of the sudden giving birth in front
of the television . . . .

Really, are you sure?

Erasures are like pillow fights
in the morning: drowsy and some-
what illicit. In the bathroom, reading
a drab translation of *Candide*. Or laying
on the knoll, herding cloud formations;
temperance succumbing to all the sick
seductions of pink field light. Undo.
Contain. Or verge.

Find piracy in the lawfully got.

Mender

We were just not meant for each other, we decided. Both of us put up a brave front about it all, but a love affair, like some prodigy of plastic surgery, is flesh laid on to living flesh and to break it up is to tear off great hunks and parts of yourself.

- William Styron

You've found home; the stereo-
typed disciples drinking Black Russians,
rapping at your doorstep.

The foundling is also a waif, a stray—
is subsidized too. You were never alerted.
Nor did you know about the legacy
chemicals locked, augered forever
in your
lungs.

It's our constant versioning, our
flicking disparity like elastics at class-
mates that sustain us. There's nothing
perilous, per se.

It's not our fault the tilt is too much—
our fault
the refrain has over-stayed
its welcome. Are we shamefaced
because we rely too heavily
on the forecast, because we
rush the muses unjustly into singing?

I know it's your first impulse
to invent—to villanize—claim
exclusivity rights when all they want
is to divvy, share. All I'm saying is

do it, but subtly, thinly. Like you aren't
even
there.

As we all take turns at the saltlick . . . .

I

As we all take turns at the saltlick,
the dolorous forms that contort
the embarrassed grass elude us.
We are far too absorbed amid the glib
transactions of slow-coming evening,
evening out our disparate heads.

II

Forget it. If you do

it will all be new
tomorrow. Songs will flood on purpose
and purpose will (peaceably) turn purposeless.

Can you wait?

III

Don't maintain for one fucking second
that a masterpiece is gestating in those
routined dreams of yours. You've neglected
the only thing that continues to save: the
footy waltz across the carpet, the scramble
of waiting, the unfashionable boundaries. Just
please, re-examine and don't just *meditate*.

IV

Okay. I've been waiting
all
night
to use the word *taciturn*—so here it is.
My eyes tonight aren't reliable guides.
I volunteered to no one. Help me.

I'm drowning. Is what you'd expect
to hear, in this *usual bazaar* of dissipating
figurines, triggering the instants that rule
the instance. My accomplice.

My page. Fray. The do-dates are all illusion.

The ballast beckoned.

There are trees there, and things.

The damned

For those of us who need the night
explained—our hearts too
bound up in sinew—those of us
who might mystify the brightest given
the chance—are soluble, unreachable,
until it's too late. Who aren't gifted
to see it.

The shelter on the lake is like paradise,
or is.

The statues align for you
(in your finery), are vested in your passable
fireworks display.

In the bath,
you've reached a certain point. In
bed your muscles ache
and miracle.

When do you draw the line between
cycle and sequence? It seems
no one is these days.

In that life

there's no time for bucolics, the ludicrous,
frozen stewardship—

> your stunning nose.

Tell me a story.

(Make it about a story) and
how there's never enough time to get it all
down.

Begin with: there's a wave.

A boot on the edge.

A wave with seniority.

Become accustomed

Come put the verb-wheel down
And kiss my mouth despite the foot in it.

- James Merrill

Our gifts (tell me, which ones?) rival
us, spurn. A growing, glowing patina
on the bronzed hall railing.

Your shoulders, barbed and seraphic.

The girl in the pyjamas who I've given
a back-story and will likely never see.

Me, the altruist-manqué.

There are worse scares: the grin
he counterfeits for social reasons,
the hawk's broad broadcast high
above the telephone pole.

Into the rift swim rivulets of
imagined paint—paint-like-air—pain-
staking; featureless, bare.

Serene is almost always profiled
as such. It's like you've said: spectres

are far from cases of mistaken identity.

And if you can't touch it, etch it out—

if it's too hard to tell whether this tryst-recital
is blind or zealless, our efforted

chorus, a synth and sized art.

Our taking pleasure in it, nearly the same.

The caption read: *heavy secret*

When the forest is not in
tune with the secret disease.

In the darling night.

There's lugubrious raining.

You will bless this *double entendre*;

hear yourself
vaulting yourself into the pit of your stomach.

Dummies wonder

To what do we owe this unfuturing,

this failing to pale our time?

Am I alone in this?—

The elliptical . . . cheering on
a dummy
dream, careening into sleep's
cabbage-role afghan. You're
not-fallen (this time)—just
under-the-bubble-bath-looking-
up.

An unjust
stomach, bloody with art: abstract
and squiggly, like the veins from run-off
on a muddy bank. And all this blood-

flow, ferrying primal fear is nothing
like dusty sunlight through barn slats.

More like a travelling circus, diverted.

So why fry the ironist, in all her
care-full uncaring? Who's unfeeling
when they yawn
over-dramatically at the cathedral?

And on the subject of death—
the horror of decomposing—the unthink-
able thought of being eaten by the world's
chemistry. We'll call it

Post-distance—invent
a new school in a wood somewhere
where dummies wonder, rummage
for rumoured streams, all parched
and far-fetched.

Everything is movies

Some days are like scares on airplanes

In the bricky distance, a hint of sunlight

Dogs meet on the street. It turns violent

Between the toes of learning

Someone said once don't hold back

Past catholic schools with weird names
like, Assumption

The obvious thing would be to cry

It's okay, your dad did it

Squirrel your earnings for the Last Chapter

What does hair have to do with pollution?

When something <u>mispells</u> itself. Dispels itself

*

The Infinite reaches infant-like for globs of
matter. The bones disappear, once. Once, our
mutualness forgave. Now it hunts for lost Frisbees
in the cedar brush, on bottle-strewn school rooftops,
with a sharp-but-perilous eye. No more playing detective,
no more inside-policing . . . no more tossing thought
to the rabid cats that own this place. There's a certain
turbulence that accompanies these veins. In short, you say,
some days are like scares on airplanes.

*

Today, a god will screen all her calls, take a bath and regret. The phone rings unceasing. In the bricky distance a hint of sunlight makes the shape of you in twenty years. The shocking image lingers in your head until it's wiped clean by commerce. You need a tree. We *all* need a tree . . . or something tree-*like*—growing and basic.

*

Outside begins to hail.
The corners are detaching; things
are getting undimensional. Shoving us off
beyond the handsome of our light. What
did you slip in my Dr. Pepper?

We leave. The barrage stops.
Dogs meet in the street. It turns
violent.

*

Your mother calls you on a false memory, lends books to dumb infants between the toes of learning on sword sharpening and shield polishing. You come across as unfeeling—reeling into hard rational bashing; you come across a fully-working shower on the curb . . . . It's these weird moments that come to terms with gorillas signing, a mountain imploding, the sun's slow kill. It's all politics: the way we anthologize the ones we wish we hadn't.

*

At the time
it didn't sink in, didn't cleave to,
when someone said once don't hold back.
It was grainy, granular,
like a fan-organ vanishing—was like
suspicious instruments made
to imitate waterfowl. And when
I heard it, I shrugged it from my immediate
being, volleyed the genius reason in-
to the fast evaporating chasm.

Call it what you will:
supra-fraternity, missed sisterhood,
creosote—
              fashioned magic.

But you are not my dangling gargoyle—my
lover-in-plastic—sparse as the defunct lacrosse
field: super-flooded by a million glittering globules.

All the while, behind my back,
conflating your masterpiece, pitted against
your shoes, in the senseless klezmer of dream.

*

It's the sad-sack trend. The motor gurgling into the night, past catholic high schools with weird names like, *Assumption*. The transom crumbles in to all light: our rarefied crosspiece disengaged—traded for holism. The two read in silence. The brain daisies when the hat is removed too soon. You check off words as they come, the catalogue completing quite self-managingly.

This is invention.

The torrid thing, un and becoming.
The coffee dregs hoping for one last oblivious gulp.

*

There's no where to go after polish: the thing
shimmers, completed. We
are left with that
and no questions

(the obvious thing would be to cry).

The rust at least bleeds, begs
for attention, says things like:
look at my ghost—look at it!
And
I call that one: Philippé's Penis.

There are things happening:
a ratified pulpit,
a crag of unadulterated longing.

A notion of several more notions.

*

The last of the solitudinarians.
The last of the sad mantelpiece.
We dropped our myriad causes

for one common cause: the contusioned
mist listlessly listening
to your giggling, your heavy breathing

into the unplugged microphone: a micro-
phone invisible, purposeless. Lost
in its own mechanism.

In your 1st-at-bat moment,
the day your prophecy self-fulfills,
the autodidact transforms

in an attenuated sort
of metamorphosis. Sirens ring . . .
the interloper psyches up

for one more daredevil act—
one more big scale.

It's okay, your dad did it.

*

The couch springs are tightly coiled
But the air is in quicker disarray

We mask our absences with loose brick
But the gadgets and tracts are heaped in hay

There's a dithering this side of *this way*
The indefatigable light is: *verity astride grey*

But the air, o the air is in quicker disarray
Yes, the air, the forced air is in quicker disarray

Squirrel your earnings for the Last Chapter
They say. Bury your bothers in somnambulant clay

For the fortified couch springs are wound, are coiled
And the breaths are short—are short and gay

When the air is in quicker disarray
When the air is in quicker disarray

*

   Every horrible era has its visitations,
every spelling error its self-correcting
posture. Am I wrong? Am I the shell
that sounds like the highway? And what
does hair have to do with pollution? The
soot puts itself in the clock's mechanism,
gives the world its thin, untimely film.

I paste a wet autumn leaf to my forehead
and walk, nonchalant, through the mall . . . .

*

Summon it up, up through the gnarly
brush, past the last blasted star. It's been
sitting on your bare shoulder all year, forever
nibbling your ear.

It's not the horror of invention. *That*
type of ascension would require wings of gel,
miniature tractor beams by the billions. It's not
the brilliant village idiot's suicide show, or the
short-listed spin-off that followed.

What you need is a good dirty talk, an impervious
walk in a gothic wood. Don't fake clandestine
when something <u>mispells</u> itself. Dispels itself.
Don't prick the visionary—or follow your new
toes to every illuminated story title. End here.

No, here. No . . .

here.

Notes

P.14- the line *Naima plays* refers to the song *Naima* by John Coltrane.

P.15- the last italicized line: *no lacking matter* is taken from Marcus McCann's poem *And snatching the broad from the building.*

P.16- the poem *Aquifer* was written by Marcus McCann in my "voice."

P.17-18- *Unnatural Speeds* is dedicated to my brother in poetic exile (i.e. the University of New Brunswick), Jesse Ferguson.

P.27- borrows a line from Joanna Newsom's song *En Gallop.*

P. 31- *Song writhing* owes a debt to the poetry of Gordon Downie and borrows some words and images.

P.34- borrows some words from Gordon Downie's poem *Starpainters.*

P.41- italicized line: *fizzy with sedatives* is from Sylvia Plath's poem *Face Lift.*

P.51- quote from the poem *Crazy Weather* by John Ashbery.

P.58- *New Illumination* is after a haunting and moving staged photograph by Gregory Crewdson.

P.59- quote from the poem *Foreboding* by John Ashbery.

P.67- title quote from the poem *1×1* by E.E. Cummings.

P.71- *Vital ORgans* appeared previously in *Bywords Quarterly Journal.*

P.73- quote from William Styron's novel *Set this House on Fire.*

P.74-75- italicized line: *usual bazaar* is from James Merrill's poem *The Friend of the Fourth Decade.*

P.78- quote from the poem *To my Greek* by James Merrill.

P.83- the concept for the *Everything is movies* sequence draws from Kevin Connolly's poem *Sestina*, where each poem in the ensuing sequence contains a different line (in sequence) from the opening collage poem.

Acknowledgments

My gratitude goes to publisher rob mclennan (fellow Glengarrian) for his support and encouragement over the years; and of course for the heaps of free poetic ephemera! Very special thanks to publisher Jennifer Mulligan for making it all happen and also letting me in on the whole process; I'm grateful.

Zealous thanks to Marcus McCann for his tireless edits and invaluable suggestions. To Genevieve Wesley for her love and support and for listening to literally each and every poem, moments after their inception. To Jesse Ferguson, my brother in poetic exile: thanks for your friendship and support. Thanks to Kevin Connolly for his own mind-blowing poetry and his more-than-helpful advice/suggested reading list.

And finally, to all my friends and family who've been so supportive or at least kept the teasing to a minimum, thank you.

Nicholas Lea was born in Whitehorse, Yukon Territory and grew up in and around the Ottawa area. He now lives and writes and works in Ottawa. He is the author of a previous chapbook entitled, light years (above/ground press) and has published his work in a number of print and online journals. For several years, he has been an active member of Ottawa's poetry community, doing readings, working with journals and participating in workshops.

Other titles from Chaudiere Books

Decalogue: ten Ottawa poets. rob mclennan, editor, 2006.
978-0-9781601-3-5

Disappointment Island. Monty Reid, poetry, 2006.
978-0-9781601-1-1

Movements in Jars. Meghan Jackson, poetry, 2006.
978-0-9781601-0-4

The Desmond Road Book of the Dead. Clare Latremouille, fiction, 2006.
978-0-9781601-2-8